Reading Essentials
in Social Studies

On Both Sides of the
Civil War

Thomas S. Owens

Perfection Learning®

With thanks to author Diana Star Helmer

Editorial Director: Susan C. Thies
Editor: Mary L. Bush

Cover Design: Michael A. Aspengren
Book Design: Deborah Lea Bell
Image Research: Lisa Lorimor

Image Credits
The Granger Collection: pp. 6, 7; Museum of the Confederacy: p. 22;
Northwind Picture Archives: pp. 5, 12–13, 34–35

ArtToday(www.arttoday.com): pp. 9, 10, 13 (inset), 14, 33; Corel: pp. 2–3 (bkgd),
4–5 (bkgd), 11 (bkgd), 14 (bkgd); ©Digital Stock: pp. 2–3, 3, 15, 21, 23, 26, 34, 38,
38–39; Emily Greazel: p. 29; Lane Studio, Gettysburg, PA: p. 6 (bkgd);
Library of Congress: pp. 1, 4–5, 8–9, 11, 16 (top), 18, 24, 27, 28, 31, 34–35 (bkgd),
36, 39 (top); National Archives: pp. 8–9 (bkgd), 10–11 (bkgd), 12–13 (bkgd),
16–17 (bkgd), 19, 20, 22–23 (bkgd), 24–25 (bkgd), 26–27 (bkgd), 29 (bkgd), 30,
32–33 (bkgd), 37, 38–39 (bkgd), 40

For information, contact
Perfection Learning® Corporation
1000 North Second Avenue, P.O. Box 500
Logan, Iowa 51546-0500.
Phone: 1-800-831-4190
Fax: 1-800-543-2745
perfectionlearning.com

2 3 4 5 6 PP 08 07 06 05 04

Paperback ISBN 0-7891-5876-0

Contents

The Battle of Shiloh was also known as the Battle of Pittsburg Landing.

Chapter 1

August 28. 1862
1862

LC-US262-3.

Too Soon

"**Conscription** agent of the **Confederacy**!"

The rumbling voice followed a pounding on the door. "May I please see the males in the household?"

Daniel Mayfield looked at his father. James Mayfield was a 45-year-old farmer. Daniel was his only child.

"Let's greet our visitor," Mr. Mayfield said.

When Daniel opened the door, he saw two men. Their horses stood behind them.

Confederate troops prepare to cross a river.

One man wore a suit and tie. He looked like a preacher. His horse looked as gray and tired as the man's beard.

Beside him stood a Confederate soldier. Daniel stared at the man wearing a gray wool uniform. Gold buttons sparkled like small suns from the soldier's jacket. Daniel couldn't help but smile at the well-dressed man.

The man's smile sparkled like his buttons. When Daniel's mother, Lilly Mayfield, came to the door, the soldier bowed.

"I'm county agent Ezra Morton," announced the other man. He removed a list from his saddlebag. "A new law orders all men ages 18 to 35 to serve in our Confederate armed forces for a period of three years."

Mrs. Mayfield stepped in front of her husband. "Mr. Morton, my husband just celebrated his forty-fifth birthday this past winter."

Confederate soldier in uniform

This wood engraving was printed in a Northern newspaper in June 1861. It shows the "drumming up" of recruits for the Confederate army in Montgomery, Alabama.

Daniel noticed that the county agent never moved. He briefly studied Mr. Mayfield's thinning gray hair. Then he turned to Daniel.

"Is this your son?" he asked.

James Mayfield edged his wife aside. "Daniel just turned 14 last week."

The Battle of Shiloh was one of the most devastating battles in American history.

"I believe he looks 18," Mr. Morton said. "Can you prove his age?"

Daniel smiled bigger. He had grown taller than his father in the past year. Not being seen as a child felt good.

The good feeling melted when his mother hissed. "Sir," she began, "I gave birth to this boy on April 15, 1848. You were not there. I was. My word is my proof."

Mr. Morton sighed. "I wish to see a family Bible or other writing to prove this young man's age."

The soldier pretended to cough. "Let me introduce myself," he said. "I am Private Samuel Winters. This month, I fought the **Union** invaders at the Battle of Shiloh. I

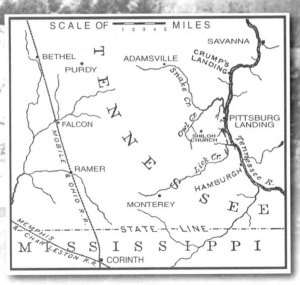

Pittsburg Landing, where the Battle of Shiloh took place, is located along the Tennessee River.

stood beside General Johnston. We faced the Northerners. They wanted to control our river, our land, and our way of life. We will keep winning until the war is over and victory is ours. Long live the South!"

Daniel and his parents smiled and nodded.

"If you don't join Private Winters and Tennessee's finest, you will be called," he said. "We need every strong male." Mr. Morton pointed at Daniel.

Mrs. Mayfield clenched her fists. "He is still a boy. You cannot have him, no matter how just your cause may be."

Private Winters and Mr. Morton mounted their horses. "Defy the law and shame the Confederacy. Your family will regret this."

The words lingered in the dust stirred up by the riders.

Daniel shook his head. His parents. The Confederacy. Who should he listen to?

Chapter 2

Bullets for Everyone

Slaves harvesting a cotton crop

"The Confederate army cannot drag my only son from me," Daniel's mother growled.

Mr. Mayfield sighed. "Fear solves nothing. We must talk to my brother before making plans."

They were on their way to see Uncle Clayton now. Daniel rode behind his parents in the back of the **flatbed** wagon. Going to see Uncle Clayton was fun. At least, it used to be. Now the visit might shape Daniel's future.

Daniel thought about how much his parents admired Uncle Clayton. Clayton's house was bigger. His farm was bigger. He had two slaves working his cotton fields. The slaves' wives did Clayton's cooking and cleaning.

The four slaves seemed content, Daniel thought. He'd never seen Uncle Clayton or his wife beat one. He'd never heard the slaves complain. But their eyes never looked happy either, he realized. Even when they smiled at him, the men had a faraway look in their eyes.

Soft sobbing sliced through the still air of the countryside. The sun reflected a silver sparkle in the weeds bordering the road.

"Stop the wagon!" Daniel begged. "It's Jeremiah Hooper."

The Hoopers lived one farm away from Daniel's uncle. Jeremiah was two years older than Daniel.

The wagon pulled to a stop beside Jeremiah.

"What's wrong?" Daniel asked. "What's on your head?"

"They sent me home," Jeremiah said, wiping tears from his face. "They want me to rest. The Union can't shoot me now."

Daniel stared at the boy he once knew. He wore gray woolen soldier's pants. But they were stained with mud and ragged at the cuffs. The sleeves were torn from his once-white shirt. Daniel saw holes and a crusty red streak on the cloth. On top of Jeremiah's head was a silver pot.

"What happened?" Daniel asked.

Mr. Mayfield patted Daniel's shoulder. "Jeremiah was at war. He must have lied about his age and joined the Confederate army," he explained.

"But what happened? What's wrong with him now?" Daniel asked again.

Jeremiah tapped the metal pot on his head. "My head had no pot at Shiloh."

"Shiloh?" Daniel held his breath. "You fought at Shiloh?"

Jeremiah gripped the pot tighter to his head. His eyes scanned the clear blue sky. He swatted the air as if bees were buzzing around him. "Bad shots. They missed again."

Jeremiah kept staring at the sky. "Blue sky, red water," he sang. "Blood from both sides filled the pond."

Mrs. Mayfield gulped. "Let us take you home, Jeremiah."

Soldiers leaving the Battle of Shiloh

"No! Keep moving. Keep low. Run, Daniel. Now!" Jeremiah warned. "There are enough bullets for everyone. Bullets don't care where you live. North or South, the bullets will find you."

Jeremiah looked around with a fearful look in his eyes. Dropping to his hands and knees, he scampered away like a dog on the run.

The Mayfields watched Jeremiah disappear over a hill. At last, Daniel's mother said, "Should we go after him? He was such a nice boy."

"It's too late for him," Mr. Mayfield declared.

No one spoke for the next hour. When their wagon pulled into the familiar drive, Daniel asked, "Have you decided what to say to Uncle Clayton?"

His father nodded. "We'll say good-bye. It's not too late for us. You'll not become the next Jeremiah."

Chapter 3

Belongings

Saying good-bye to Uncle Clayton may be harder than fighting Union troops, Daniel thought.

Uncle Clayton and Daniel's father were arguing loudly. Daniel knew not to interrupt his father, but Uncle Clayton spoke his mind whenever he felt like it.

"I am good to my slaves!" Clayton roared at James. "I bought them with money I earned. The Union wants to punish me for working hard. They want to take what's mine. And you want to help them by not allowing your son to help in the fight!"

Uncle Clayton did more than

yell. He kept poking his finger into James's shoulder. James just ignored his brother's pushing and shouting.

"Clayton, please care for our farm while we're gone," Daniel's father said calmly. "We're going to Uncle Henry's farm near Mayfield, Kentucky. It's just over the Tennessee state line. There's no forced service in Kentucky. They're a **neutral** state. If we're lucky, they'll stay that way. No one will force Daniel to fight there. We'll stay until this war is settled."

"Fine. Good-bye then." Uncle Clayton's eight stomps and one door slamming were the last sounds Daniel heard before they left.

Uncle Clayton would keep his word. He would care for his brother's farm. But Daniel knew his uncle was set on being unhappy about it.

Many families had to leave their homes during the war.

The Civil War finally came to an end when General Lee surrendered to General Grant on April 9, 1865, at Appomattox Court House, Virginia.

OHIO

INDIANA

WEST VIRGINIA

ILLINOIS

KENTUCKY

VIRGINIA

MISSOURI

UNION

CONFEDERACY

TENNESSEE

NORTH CAROLINA

ARKANSAS

←Tennessee River

Shiloh Church★ ★Pittsburg Landing

SOUTH CAROLINA

ALABAMA

GEORGIA

MISSISSIPPI

Late into the night, Daniel and his parents crammed their wagon with blankets, pans, dishes, and the few clothes they owned.

"This war will be over soon," Mrs. Mayfield said hopefully.

Daniel and his father stopped. They smiled at her. But neither had the strength or hope to nod their agreement.

At sunrise, they started north.

"Lilly and Daniel," Mr. Mayfield ordered, "keep watch for soldiers in any uniform. If you see them, let me know."

"Yes, sir." Daniel saluted his father and grinned. But his father's frown only grew. Daniel decided his family might not feel like laughing for a long time to come.

Daniel perched in the back of the wagon and kept a close watch on their belongings. Which chair would be the first to topple over the edge of the crowded wagon? Which basket would leap out at the next turn? After each bump, he patted and pushed everything back in place.

Daniel's heart jumped when their wagon topped a hill. He saw two black boys huddled beside a bush. They weren't soldiers. Were they slaves?

Daniel didn't want to alert his father. James Mayfield owned no slaves. But Daniel wasn't sure if his father would help runaways. After all, someone had paid a lot of money for them.

Daniel didn't want to stop either. He wanted a quiet, fast trip to a safer town. Mayfield had been named after his relatives who had settled the town. No one would question a Mayfield in Mayfield.

Daniel could see now that the two boys were about his age.

He looked at his parents in the front seat of the wagon. They were whispering about life in Kentucky. They never saw the boys frozen with fear under the bush.

Daniel waved at the boys. He picked up two apples and held them up. Then he tossed each apple toward the bush. Daniel saw two dark brown hands pop out from the bush. They snatched the apples before they hit the ground.

After the wagon passed the bush, Daniel wanted to do more. Without a word, he dropped two empty **burlap** bags in the dirt road. His mother had brought extras. The cloth could be used as a blanket, a shirt, or a bag to carry things.

As the wagon topped a hill, Daniel saw the runaways appear. Small and faraway, they plucked their presents from the dirt. Both boys saluted. Daniel couldn't help but chuckle softly as his unknown friends ran back to their bushy hideout.

Escaped slaves who joined the Union forces were called *contrabands*.

Chapter 4

Whose War Is It?

An hour later, the Mayfields spotted a stranger marching down the road toward them.

"I'll grab the frying pan, just in case," Mrs. Mayfield said.

"No need," Daniel said. "He looks unarmed."

The stranger waved. "Can you help a hungry farm boy?"

The stranger dusted off his ragged wool clothes. Daniel's eyes bulged. How could the soldier wear a Confederate gray jacket *and* Union blue pants?

"Good day, sir," Daniel's father said. "Whose uniform do you wear?"

"That depends on the pay." The man grinned. "I am Robert Blankenship. I come from Burlington, Iowa, on the Mississippi River. I came in search of excitement."

Mrs. Mayfield cleared her throat. She passed him a couple of apples and asked, "Does your hometown mean you fight to preserve the Union?"

"I don't think the Union needs me," Robert said. "I think the South will beat itself."

"I'm afraid I don't understand," Mrs. Mayfield said.

"Do you know of the Twenty Negro Rule?" Robert asked. "The wealthy Southern farmers sure do! An owner or **overseer** of twenty slaves gets to stay home from the war."

The dusty, oddly dressed soldier shrugged. "It's a rich man's war but a poor man's fight. Well, this is one poor man who's looking for pay. I'll fight on the side that can afford me."

Daniel's father snorted. "You *must* be from the North. Southerners wouldn't fight against their own people."

"The Confederate army has attacked its own soldiers with the conscription law," Robert replied. "All the men and boys in the army thought they could go home after one year of service. Now the army has passed a law forcing those soldiers to stay for two more years."

"So it's true," said Mr. Mayfield.

"It gets worse," Robert warned. "Confederate officers fear all their soldiers will **desert**. So they're shooting men who protest the law. They're shooting their own men!"

Mrs. Mayfield moaned.

Daniel looked at the soldier. "How old are you? Are you over 18?"

"I'm old enough," Robert said.

Daniel handed him another apple. "Where are you going now?"

"I'm off to join the army."

Daniel's father scratched his head. "But you're wearing a uniform. Aren't you already in the army?"

Robert winked and flashed another huge smile. "I get a $300 bonus each time I volunteer. After a while, I get lost and then rejoin another unit. I use different names to sign up, of course."

Mrs. Mayfield shook her finger at him. "Young man, do not be proud of lying!"

Robert's smile disappeared. "I am proud of staying alive, ma'am. And I am proud I have not wasted my life on this senseless war. *My* blood alone cannot make a second country for the South. My bullets cannot end slavery for the North."

Daniel had never met anyone like this soldier. His face was young, but his eyes were so old.

Robert Blankenship managed

one last small, tired smile. "Thank you for your kindness. Take care of yourselves. I must be going."

The family waved good-bye. They continued following the Tennessee River north to Kentucky.

Daniel closed his eyes. He thought of all the people he'd seen who had been changed by this new war. But they were just individuals. Could a whole country ever change? And if it did, would it be for the better or the worse?

Chapter 5

What Remains?

That night, the Mayfields parked the wagon under a huge oak tree near the road. In the morning, the wagon lumbered down the road again. After a mile or so, Daniel saw two men sleeping on the side of the road. At least, he hoped they were sleeping.

As they drew closer, Daniel spotted the uniforms both wore. The men were from opposite sides. One wore a Confederate jacket, while the other was dressed in Union gray.

"Good heavens!" Mrs. Mayfield whispered. "It's that Robert Blankenship boy."

Confederate soldier

Confederate prisoners under guard at an encampment

Daniel's stomach knotted. His father stopped the wagon. Daniel jumped down and bent over the boy. He passed his hand over Robert's face, closing the soldier's eyes.

"I think he was shot in the back," Daniel's father said. "I don't think he saw it coming."

Daniel's mother knelt beside the body to pray. Daniel turned to look at the second body.

"A Union soldier?" Daniel asked. "Weren't they on the same side?"

"No," Daniel's father answered. "Robert wanted no side. This soldier may have been sent to bring Robert back to his unit. He would have been disappointed to find him dressed in Confederate colors."

Daniel gasped. "But how could Robert have killed him? He had his back turned."

Daniel's father shrugged. "It could've been anyone. We're still in a Confederate state." He pulled a shovel from the wagon. "We need to bury both bodies and be on our way."

Most of a soldier's pay was spent at a sutler's tent or wagon. Items such as sardines, canned peaches, and condensed milk were sold at extremely high prices, so cash didn't last long.

"A wagon!" Mrs. Mayfield pointed. Daniel quickly covered the dead faces with burlap.

The wagon was huge. It could carry the belongings of many families, Daniel thought. As the wagon drew closer, Daniel saw caps, bags, and other packages hanging on nails from the sides of the wagon. One board listed prices. It wasn't a wagon of family belongings—it was a store on wheels!

"Horace Hickman, sutler!" called the driver.

Daniel frowned. "What's a sutler?"

"I am an official supplier to a **regiment** of soldiers," Hickman answered. "They choose what they need, and I credit them. Their debts are taken from their pay."

Daniel's father turned a shovel of dirt for the first grave. "I think you lost a couple of customers here, sir. We discovered their bodies after the fight."

"You're not going to bury them like that, are you?" Hickman asked.

"Why?" Mrs. Mayfield asked. "Is there a better way?"

Hickman motioned for Daniel and Mr. Mayfield to come closer. "Pardon us, ma'am," he said. "This isn't the sort of talk ladies should hear."

He put a hand on Mr. Mayfield's shoulder. "You found them, so I'll make you a deal. I'll pay you half of what I'll make."

Mr. Mayfield stared. "I don't understand."

"I can use his rifle," Hickman said, pointing at the Union soldier. Hickman dug in his pockets. Daniel heard coins clinking. "And I can use the Confederate buttons and the Union belt buckle."

"Use?" Daniel felt a chill. "What do you mean?"

Besides supplying goods to soldiers, wagons were used to deliver mail to military camps.

Hickman shrugged. "Some soldiers need to replace goods. Others want a souvenir—an item owned by the enemy. All come to me to buy."

Daniel reached for the Union soldier's rifle. He pointed the needlelike bayonet at the sutler. "Shall we test the sharpness of this weapon first, sir?"

Hickman choked out a tiny, high-pitched laugh. "You'd better be careful, boy. You could hurt somebody."

Daniel felt like a dog ready to bite. "That somebody is you," he growled. "You're a **vulture** picking over dead bodies. You bring shame to your country. Leave while you still can."

Horace Hickman snapped the reins. His wagon lurched. "You Southerners will be sorry!" he yelled over the racket of the wheels.

Daniel stood guard over Robert Blankenship's body until the sutler was just a dot on the hilltop. Then he turned to face his parents.

"That was brave," Daniel's father said. His mother nodded in agreement, though her eyes held fear. Bravery could get a boy killed in this war.

Daniel dropped the rifle. He dropped to his knees beside the grave.

His tears couldn't wash away Robert's blood. Wiping his eyes, Daniel looked at Robert's calm face. The soldier felt no more pain. For him, the war was over.

But Daniel felt as if his heart had been struck by a cannonball.

Chapter 6

Bury Me Not

The Mayfields stopped their wagon on a high ridge. "I wish we could see Kentucky from here," Mr. Mayfield sighed.

Daniel pointed. "Look! Troops approaching! Maybe a dozen on horseback. They look like Union troops!"

His parents froze in fear. Only Daniel kept moving. Now was no time for panic.

"Lie flat in the wagon back. Remove your boots!" Daniel ordered his father. "Cover him with burlap, Mother! Everything but his feet. Hurry!"

A company of Union soldiers drilling in formation

This man is being punished for stealing from a wounded soldier.

Daniel produced a blue Union cap from under the wagon seat.

"You took that from the dead man?" his mother asked.

"I took protection," Daniel said. He dropped the cap on top of his father.

Horses thundered closer. "Cry, Mother!" Daniel commanded.

Mrs. Mayfield put her face in her hands and moaned.

"Excuse me," an officer in blue asked. "We're missing a man. We sent him to search for a runaway. If our man has been harmed, we will find who is to blame."

The words chilled Daniel. They must be searching for the man who had died with Robert. When they found him, they might blame Daniel's family for the death.

"Sir, I beg you to let us continue on," Daniel said. "My father died to preserve this Union. We want to take him home to Kentucky to bury him."

Two Union soldiers had dismounted behind the Mayfield wagon. They noticed the familiar blue cap on top of the covered body. They bowed their heads in respect.

"Forgive me," the officer said. "I am sorry."

Mrs. Mayfield peeked from behind her hands. "We understand," she sniffled. "But we must go."

The officer held up one hand to

stop the wagon. "Wait!" he shouted. "I have an idea. Three of our men died this past week. They fell ill from drinking bad water. We buried them at our camp up yonder near the woods. Let us bury your husband there too. He's another Union hero."

This idea made Daniel's mother shriek louder than ever.

"Thank you," Daniel blurted. He thought fast. "But Father's last wish was to be buried at the family plot in Kentucky," he fibbed calmly.

The officer paused and saluted. "Very well," he announced. "The United States thanks you. Good day!"

Daniel whipped the reins, and their wagon rumbled off.

"It's safe now," his mother said after a while. "They're out of sight."

Daniel's father sat up in the wagon back. "It's good to be alive again," he laughed. "Thank you for not burying me alive!"

Daniel's mother laughed too. "That officer nearly scared the life out of me. He would have killed your father with his kindness!"

Daniel stashed the blue Union cap back under the wagon seat. Mr. Mayfield tilted his head. He reached under the seat and pulled the blue cap out again. Along with it came Robert Blankenship's gray **kepi**.

"What's this?" he asked Daniel.

Daniel cleared his throat. "The cap couldn't help Robert anymore," he explained. "But I thought it may be of help to us. If we'd met up with Southern troops, you would have been wearing that cap."

Both parents looked at each other. Then they looked at Daniel and laughed.

Mr. Mayfield slapped his son on the back. "Our boy could talk the white stripe off a skunk," he said.

Daniel laughed the loudest of all. Laughing felt so much better than crying.

As they reached a crossroad, Daniel spotted another reason for joy. He read the sign ahead of them out loud.

Chapter 7

Lessons to Learn

After a week of sleeping on the ground, Daniel spent the night on Great-Aunt Mabel's **feather tick mattress**. The next morning, he had his first bath in a week. Jumping into the Tennessee River to cool off hadn't been the same.

After dressing in clean clothes, Daniel explored the countryside. Kentucky seemed like a dream. He hadn't seen a single man in uniform yet.

Daniel spotted a small building on top of the hill facing Mabel and Henry's farm.

"What is that **whitewashed** building standing all alone?" Daniel asked his Great-Uncle Henry. "Is it a barn without a farmhouse?"

Henry Mayfield shook his head. "The place is nothing now. It used to be our country church. But our minister and the men from most families have gone to fight. I'm proud that three out of every four chose the Union side. Still, church in an empty building makes for a sad service."

Daniel fell asleep that night with the word *service* buzzing in his head. An empty church service. The Confederate Armed Services. Being of service.

Daniel wanted to be of service in this confusing time. He wanted to feel as if he were doing something. But, as Robert Blankenship had said, how could his blood or bullets change the world? Could there be a better answer?

By the next morning, Daniel had found his answer.

"Mother, you and Father have taught me well," he said. "I want to share what I've learned with others. I can be of service to my country by teaching the children of Mayfield what I know."

He told his mother and father about the empty church. "Children can come to school in the old building," he said. "What else do the children have to do right now? They can do more than wait for bullets and death."

"I should warn you, Daniel," his father said. "Being a teacher keeps you out of forced military service in Tennessee. Some here might claim you want to teach only to avoid fighting."

Daniel snorted. "Bravery isn't only on the battlefields. It can be found in the classroom as well. Teaching children to read and write and think is the hope of our future. What could be a better cause?"

Daniel set his plan into motion the next day. He walked from farm to farm, knocking on doors. He told families about his new school. He promised it would be free to anyone who came. But if anyone wanted to pay him, he added with a smile, he wouldn't complain.

"Would this be a school for **Yankee** or Confederate children?" One man growled at him.

Daniel didn't back down. "I will teach all children. I won't teach them to be Northerners or Southerners. I'll teach them to be thinking, caring people."

For a week, Daniel told families that school would begin on Monday. That Saturday, he swept out the church and washed its two windows. He set his great-uncle's goat grazing in front of the new school.

"What good is having students if they get lost in the grass?" he asked the goat.

Monday morning, Daniel said good-bye to his family minutes after sunrise. He ran up the hill to his new schoolhouse. He opened the front door and waited.

And waited.

Aside from a screeching blue jay, Daniel was alone. He sat in the front of the church until lunchtime, ready to greet students.

As Daniel finished the lunch he'd brought in a pail, he heard quiet footsteps.

"Are you the teacher?" squeaked a boy. "I'm sorry I'm late. I had to herd our cows back home this morning."

Daniel leaped to his feet. "That's quite all right. And, yes, I am the teacher. I'm Mr. Mayfield. Who are you?"

The boy saluted. "George Wilson, sir."

Daniel smiled. "First lesson. This is not the army." He shook George's hand.

Daniel and George went inside together, leaving the Civil War outside where it belonged.

Shiloh Church

Shiloh

In the Hebrew language, *Shiloh* means "a place of peace." But in April 1862, Shiloh Church was far from a peaceful place. The worst battle Americans had ever known took place around this little Tennessee church.

America had been divided for almost a year. Eleven southern states had **seceded** on May 6, 1861. They left the United States to form the Confederate States of America, a new country where slavery was allowed. That was the beginning of the Civil War.

Almost one year later, Confederate General Albert Johnston launched a surprise attack on Union soldiers. The soldiers were camped at Pittsburg Landing near the Tennessee River and Shiloh Church.

The recapture of artillery (weapons
by Union soldiers

Ulysses S. Grant

Another officer tried to talk General Johnston out of attacking Union General Grant's forces.

"I would fight them if they were a million," Johnston promised. "Tonight we will water our horses in the Tennessee."

Johnston's morning raid almost destroyed the Union camp. But the Northerners kept control of one sunken road. They had the help of an Illinois regiment and Iowa farm boys commanded by General Benjamin Prentiss.

Trying to take back the road, the Confederates attacked 11 times. They lined up 62 cannons to fire at close range. So many bullets swarmed around the Union soldiers that they called the spot "the hornet's nest." Finally, after six hours, the South overran the area and captured the road again.

That night, it rained. The rain helped hide the arrival of more Union troops and **gunboats**. By the next morning, the Union had regained control over much of the area.

Across farm fields and forests, the two armies fought for nearly 48 hours. Both sides were exhausted. When the Confederates retreated, the North did not chase them.

Soldiers who survived the Battle of Shiloh told stories of all the dead. Bodies littered the ground, they said. Walking without stepping on a fallen soldier was impossible.

One battle happened in a peach orchard. The trees were flowering. By the battle's end, the trees were bare. All the blossoms had been blown off by gunfire. The blossoms covered the dead like a blanket of snow.

Nearly 3,500 men died at Shiloh. More than 24,000 were injured. Of the 63,000 Northern troops, 1,754 were killed, and more than 13,000 were injured. Out of the 40,000 on the Confederate side, 1,728 were killed, and 11,000 were injured.

Yet, for many soldiers, the biggest worry was illness. Union soldiers jokingly called one common sickness the "Tennessee quick step." But diarrhea, **typhoid**, **dysentery**, and other illnesses were no joke. By the end of the Civil War, more men had died from diseases than from war wounds.

By the end of the Civil War in 1865, more than 600,000 Americans had died. Nearly one million suffered serious injuries.

Four years after the Battle of Shiloh, the Shiloh National Cemetery was dedicated. Soldiers from both sides—6,800 in all—are buried there. Many of them died in the Battle of Shiloh. Never before had a battle been so costly to Americans.

Field hospitals were set up near battle lines so the wounded could be cared for.

Forced to Fight

The Conscription Act was another name for the Confederate draft. This law forced Southern white men to join the Confederate army. But even though the Confederate states were supposed to stick together, some governors didn't want their men going away to fight. They wanted their **militias** to stay and defend their own states.

In places like Georgia and North Carolina, a false list of **civil servants** was used. Men on the list were excused from the draft so they could help run the state. But none of the listed men really had state jobs.

Men in other fields could also avoid the Confederate draft. Factory or railroad workers, teachers, mail carriers, and newspaper editors did not have to fight.

When the Union draft started a year later, men from the North were allowed to pay a $300 fee to the government to avoid the draft. Other men hired substitutes to go to war in their place.

The Civil War made life especially hard for people in border states. These states were caught between the Southern slave states and the Northern free states. In Missouri, 100,000 citizens fought for the Union. But 40,000 chose to serve in the Confederacy. In Kentucky, nearly 75,000 people served in the Union forces, while 25,000 were Confederate soldiers.

Only the Union side kept track of its youngest soldiers. Out of 2.7 million Union soldiers, more than 2 million were ages 18–21. More than 1 million were 16–18. Approximately 100,000 were 14 and 15 years old. A total of 300 were ages 11–13. Two dozen soldiers for the North were age 10 or under.

Most of the youngest began in the Union military as drummers or **fife** players. It's estimated that the Union forces used 40,000 musicians. These positions were ideal for young boys.

Both sides claimed that musicians were "noncombatants," or soldiers who didn't fight in armed battles. But musicians were troop leaders. A military commander expected his drummer to pound out signals to the men. The drummer would stay near his commander in order to receive messages. The other side knew that killing a drummer could stop a commander from signaling his group of men.

The most famous young soldier may have been Johnny Clem. A nine-year-old

Johnny Clem

runaway, Clem enlisted in the 22nd Michigan Regiment as a drummer. At the Battle of Shiloh, a cannon blast destroyed his drum. He grabbed a rifle and began shooting. He was nicknamed "Johnny Shiloh."

The story of Clem's bravery helped recruit more soldiers for the Union. Clem was **promoted** twice before being **discharged** in 1864.

No one knows the exact number of boys in the Confederate forces. There is record of George S. Lamkin of Winona, Mississippi. He joined the Mississippi **Battery** when he was 11. Before he was 12, Lamkin was wounded at Shiloh.

Thirteen-year-old T. G. Bean was from Pickensville, Alabama. He organized two **companies** of Confederate soldiers at the University of Alabama in 1861.

By 1864, the Confederacy drafted 17-year-olds. But most boys in uniform were volunteers. They chose to fight for their side despite the dangers.

The Civil War took the lives of thousands of Northern and Southern young men. Never again would so many young Americans take such an active part in a war.

Glossary

battery unit of soldiers

burlap heavy, woven material

civil servant person who works for the government

company unit of soldiers

Confederacy Southern side during the Civil War

conscription forcing people to join the military

desert to leave military service without leave, or permission

discharged released from service

dysentery severe stomach disease

feather tick mattress mattress made of a fabric case (tick) filled with feathers

fife small flute

flatbed having a flat surface to haul things on

gunboat armed boat

kepi military cap with a round, flat top and a visor

militia body of citizens organized for military service

neutral not taking sides

overseer person in charge of slaves on a farm

promoted moved to a higher or better position

regiment unit of soldiers

seceded left the Union of the United States

typhoid disease marked by fever, headache, and upset stomach

Union Northern side during the Civil War

vulture bird that eats the flesh of dead animals

whitewashed covered with a liquid mixture used to whiten surfaces

Yankee person who lived in the northern United States